Adult Coloring Book

100 Mandalas

An Adult Coloring Book Featuring 100 Of The Most Beautiful Mandalas For Stress Relief And Relaxation

This Book Belongs To

....

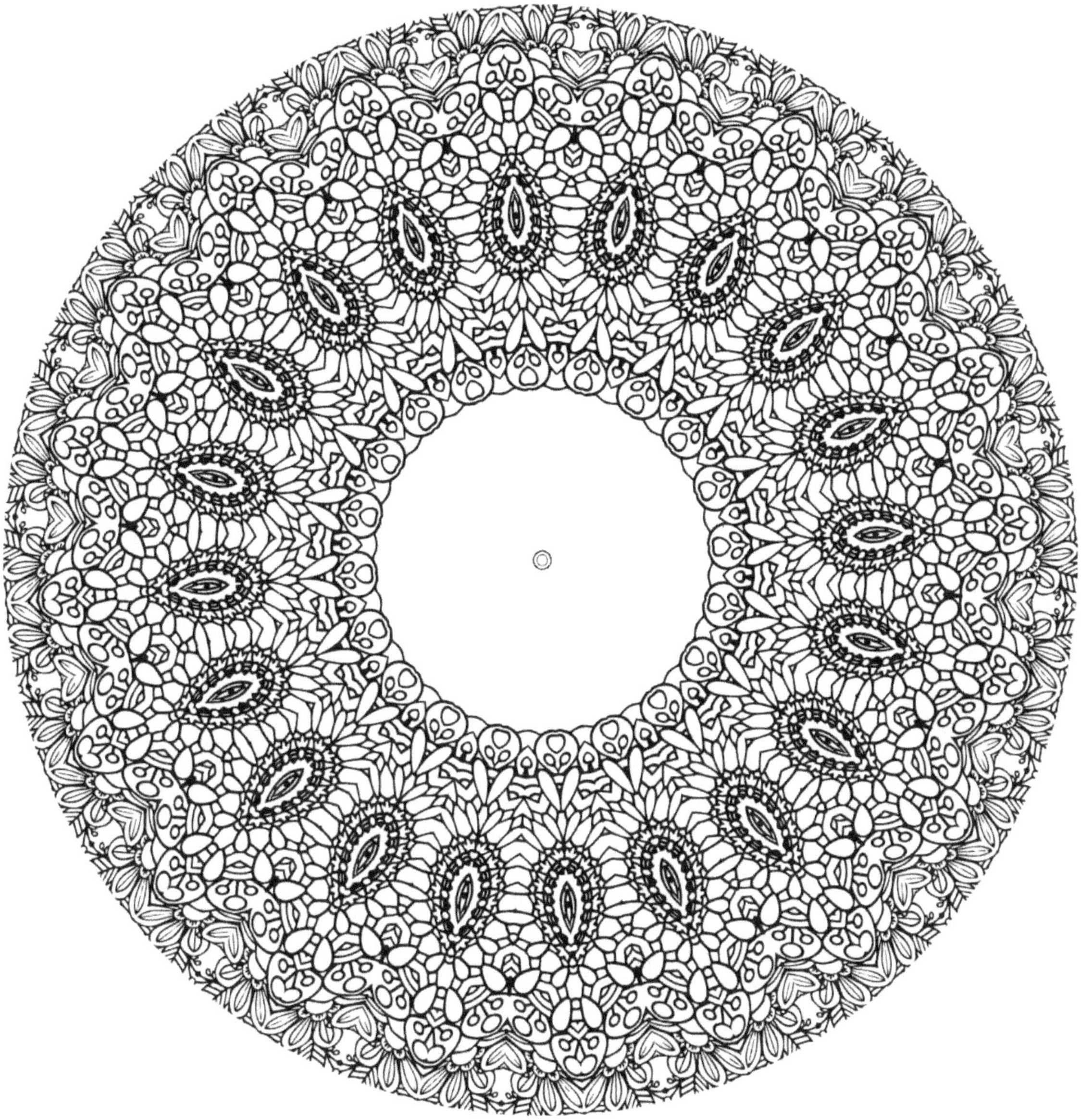

www.ingramcontent.com/pod-product-compliance
Lightning Source LLC
Chambersburg PA
CBHW082335270726
48658CB00017B/2848